Alfred's Basic Piano Library

Piano

Recital Book • Level 1A

This RECITAL BOOK may be begun when the student has reached *JOLLY OLD SAINT NICHOLAS,* on page 15 of LESSON BOOK 1A.

The pieces in this book are coordinated PAGE BY PAGE with the materials in the LESSON BOOK. They should be assigned in accordance with the instructions in the upper right corner of each page of this book. Under no circumstances should they be assigned sooner than these references indicate, although they may be assigned as review material at any time after the student has reached the page designated.

These pieces serve several important purposes:

- They provide reinforcement for every principle and concept introduced in the lesson material. (This is further reinforced through the use of the THEORY BOOK.)

- They provide extra material for students who move faster than others in class work.

- They provide highly motivating solo material, particularly effective for use in student recitals.

The last pieces in this book may be assigned as the student progresses into LESSON BOOK 1B. They will make the transition from book to book very smooth, especially since the first pages of 1B are concerned with reviewing the principles taught at 1A level.

A glance at the contents will show the great variety of selections included, some of which are intended as purely recreational, while others are deliberately challenging. Not every student should be required to learn them all, but any student who does so will find the time well spent and the results rewarding.

Willard A. Palmer • Morton Manus • Amanda Vick Lethco

A General MIDI disk ▦ is available (8588), which includes a full piano recording and background accompaniment.

Second Edition

2

Echo Song

BEGIN WITH LEFT HAND

DUET PART: Student plays 1 octave higher than shown above,
unless DUET PART is played on a 2nd piano.

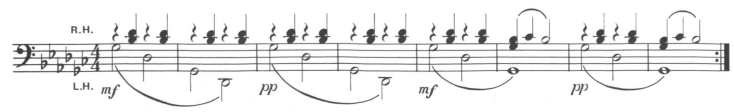

Use after JOLLY OLD SAINT NICHOLAS (page 15)
or OLD MACDONALD (page 17).

Sailor Jack

BEGIN WITH RIGHT HAND

R.H. 4 2   R.H. 2 2 4   4 2   R.H. 2 3 2

L.H. 2 3   L.H. 2 3

1. Sail - or Jack, where   have you been?   'Round the world and   back a - gain!
2. When will you be   sail - ing back?   Soon as moth - er   packs my sack!

R.H. 4 2   R.H. 2 2 4   4 2   R.H. 2 3 2

L.H. 2 3   L.H. 2 3

Sail - or Jack, how   did you sail?   Rode up - on a   hump - back whale!
How'll you sail back   Sail - or Jack?   In my dad's new   Cad - il - lac!

DUET PART: (Student plays on black-key groups **ABOVE** the middle of the keyboard.)

Rhythmically

(Play this line 4 times!)

Use after BATTER UP (page 20).

MIDDLE C POSITION

THUMBS on MIDDLE C

Strange Story

Mysteriously!

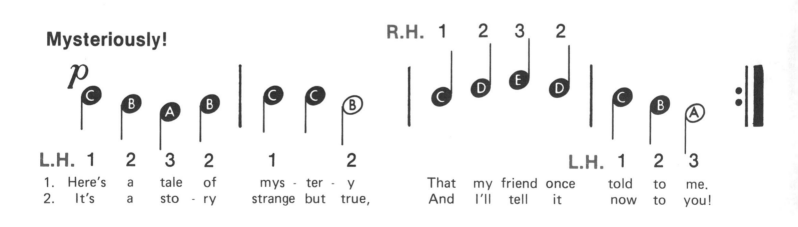

1. Here's a tale of mys - ter - y That my friend once told to me.
2. It's a sto - ry strange but true, And I'll tell it now to you!

DUET PART: (Student plays 1 octave higher.)

Use after MY CLEVER PUP (page 21).

MIDDLE C POSITION

L.H. = 4 3 2 ① 2 3 4 = R.H.

The Joke's on Us!

Brightly!

1. Ha, ha, ha, ha!   Ha, ha, ha, ha!   Ha, ha, ha, the   joke's on   you!
2. Ha, ha, ha, ha!   Ha, ha, ha, ha!   Ha, ha, ha, and   on   me,   too!

DUET PART: (Student plays 1 octave higher.)

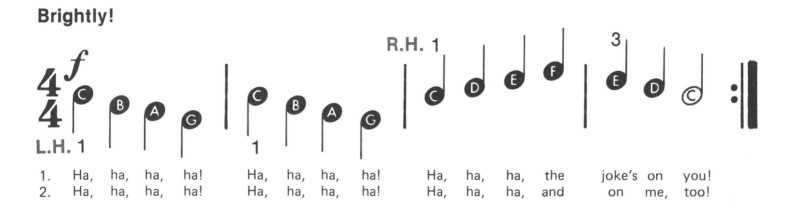

6

Use after THE ZOO (page 22).

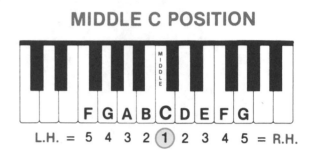

Lost My Partner!

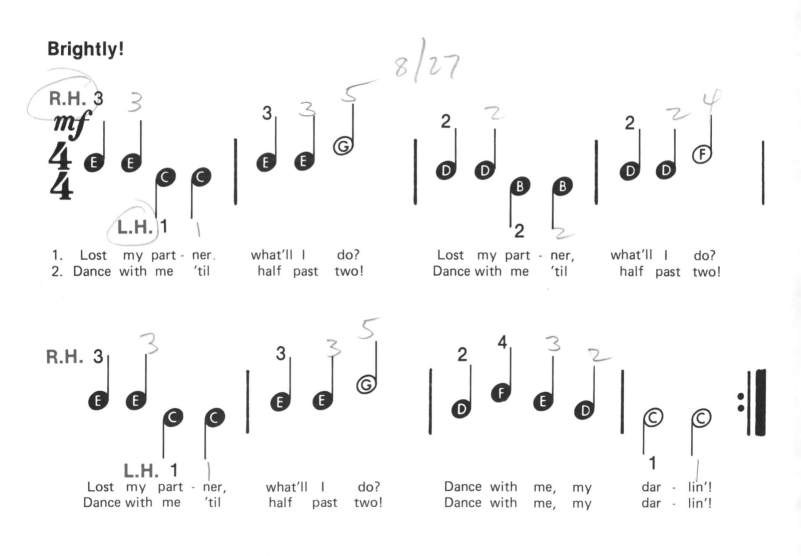

DUET PART: (Student plays 1 octave higher than shown above, unless DUET PART is played on a 2nd piano.)

Use after THE ZOO (page 22).

Old Joe Clark

MIDDLE C POSITION

Brightly!

1. Old Joe Clark, the preach-er's son, He came by one day;
2. "Fare thee well now, old Joe Clark, Fare thee well, I say!

Ate up all my chick-en fry;
"Fare thee well now, old Joe Clark!

Threw the bones a - way!
Don't come back some day!"

DUET PART: (Student plays 1 octave higher, unless DUET PART is played on a 2nd piano.)

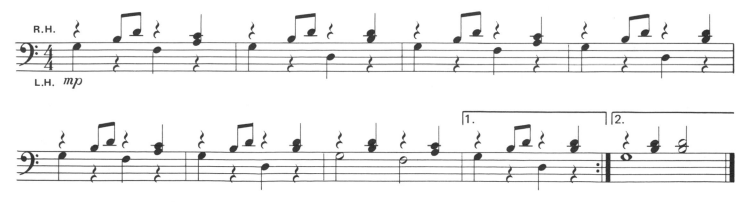

Use after PLAYING IN A NEW POSITION (page 23).

Morning Prayer

Moderately slow

C POSITION

1. Fa - ther, we thank Thee for this fine day.
2. Help us to love and to give and share.

Help us to grow as we work and play.
In Thy to dear name now we make our prayer!

A - men, A - men!

DUET PART: (Student plays 2 octaves higher.)

Use after SAILING (page 24), or SKATING (page 25).

Sunshine!

C POSITION

Happily!

DUET PART: (Student plays 1 octave higher.)

10

Use after WISHING WELL (page 26).

My Favorite Day!

C POSITION

Repeat p, if you wish!

DUET PART: (Student plays 2 octaves higher.)

Optional: Repeat more softly.

Use after RAIN, RAIN (page 29).

Mrs. Murphy's House

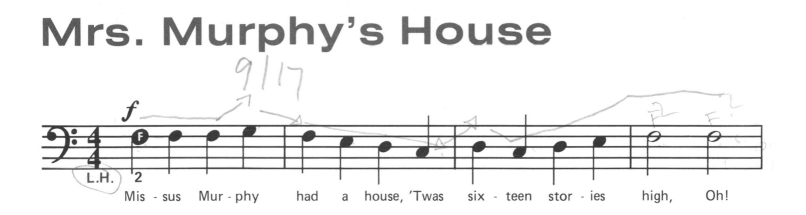

Mis - sus Mur - phy had a house, 'Twas six - teen stor - ies high, Oh!

Ev - 'ry sto - ry in that house was filled with chick - en pie, Oh!

DUET PART:

Gee, We're Glad!

Use after A HAPPY SONG (page 31).

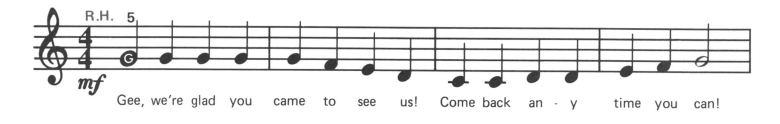

Gee, we're glad you came to see us! Come back an - y time you can!

Gee, we love to have you vis - it! Please come back a - gain!

DUET PART:

Use after A HAPPY SONG (page 34).

Christopher Columbus

C POSITION

Moderately fast

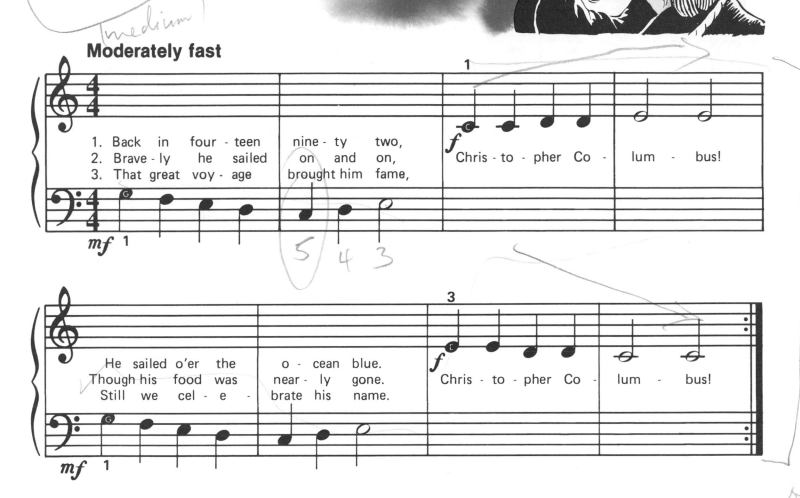

1. Back in four-teen nine-ty two, Chris-to-pher Co - lum - bus!
2. Brave-ly he sailed on and on,
3. That great voy-age brought him fame,

He sailed o'er the o-cean blue. Chris-to-pher Co - lum - bus!
Though his food was near-ly gone.
Still we cel-e - brate his name.

With the Ni - na and the Pin - ta and the St. Mar - i - a, too;

Repeat the 1st 2 lines (3rd verse).

DUET PART: (Student plays 1 octave higher.)

Fine

D.C. al Fine

Use after BALLOONS (page 37).

Come Fly!

Brightly 10/29/16

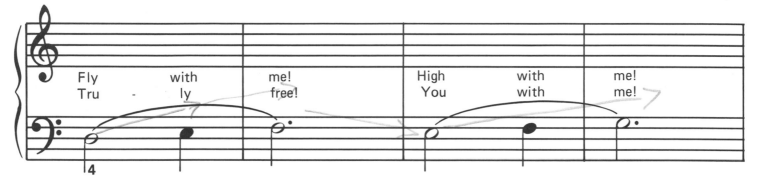

1. Come sail in the sky with me!
2. Like birds in the sky blue we'll be

Fly with me! High with me!
Tru - ly free! You with me!

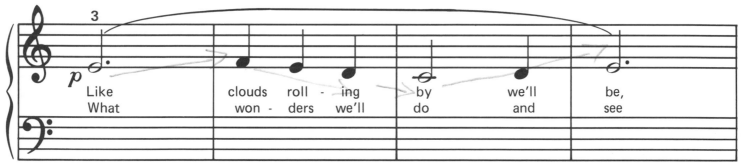

Like clouds roll - ing by we'll be,
What won - ders we'll do and see

In our beau - ti - ful plane! _____

DUET PART: (Student plays 1 octave higher.)

Robin Hood

Use after WHO'S ON 3RD (page 38)
or MEXICAN HAT DANCE (page 39).

Moderately fast

1. When will we get mar - ried, mar - ried, mar - ried?
2. Who'll come to the wed - ding, wed - ding, wed - ding?

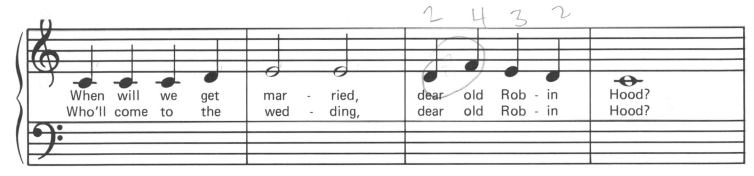

When will we get mar - ried, dear old Rob - in Hood?
Who'll come to the wed - ding, dear old Rob - in Hood?

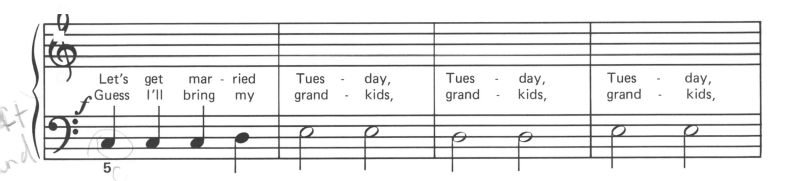

Let's get mar - ried Tues - day, Tues - day, Tues - day,
Guess I'll bring my grand - kids, grand - kids, grand - kids,

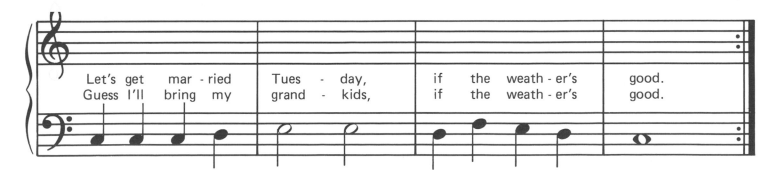

Let's get mar - ried Tues - day, if the weath - er's good.
Guess I'll bring my grand - kids, if the weath - er's good.

DUET PART: (Student plays both hands 1 octave higher.)

Play 4 times!

16

Use after ROCKETS (page 42)
or SEA DIVERS (page 43).

Quiet River

11/12/16

Moderately slow

Peace - ful riv - er, qui - et riv - er, gent - ly you flow.

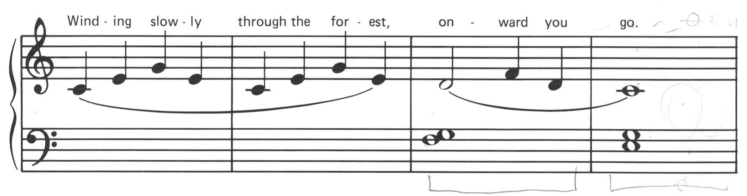

Wind - ing slow - ly through the for - est, on - ward you go.

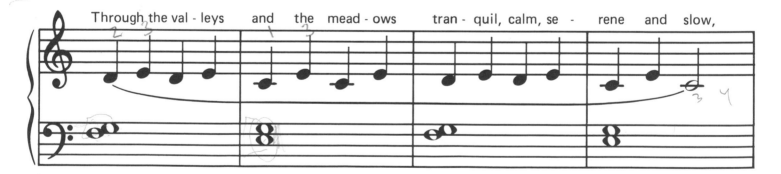

Through the val - leys and the mead - ows tran - quil, calm, se - rene and slow,

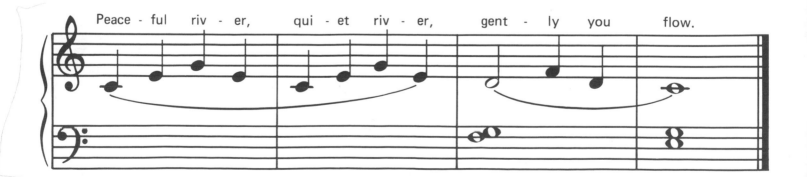

Peace - ful riv - er, qui - et riv - er, gent - ly you flow.

Use after JULY THE FOURTH (page 45).

Come to My House!

18

Use after LOVE SOMEBODY (page 47).

The Call of the Horn

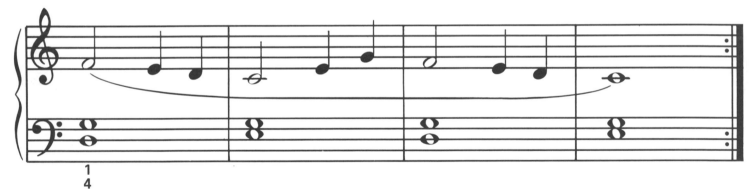

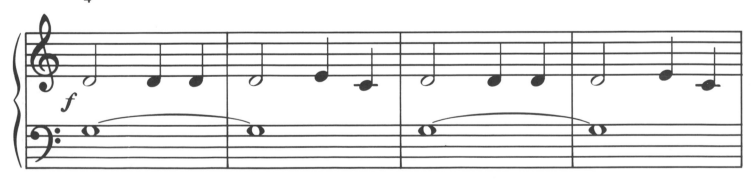

Play the 1st 2 lines twice more, *f - p*.

Rock Anywhere!

Use after MY FIFTH (page 48).

Moderately fast

1. Rock can be found in a tune!
2. Some like to rock in a boat!

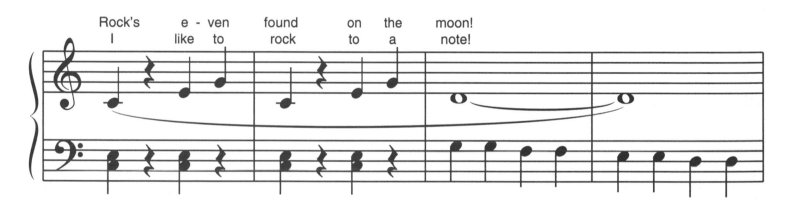

Rock's e - ven found on the moon!
I like to found rock on to the a moon! note!

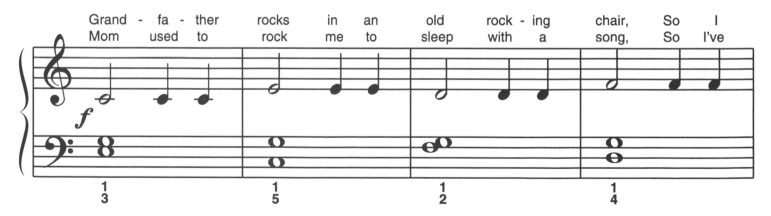

Grand - fa - ther rocks in an old rock - ing chair, So I
Mom used to rock me to sleep with a song, So I've

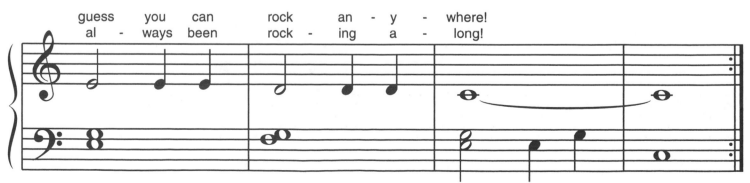

guess you can rock an - y - where!
al - ways been rock - ing a - long!

20

Use after THE DONKEY (page 49).

Favorite Words

Gently

Some of my fa - vor - ite words be - gin with

"G!"

Glis - ten and glim - mer and glow,

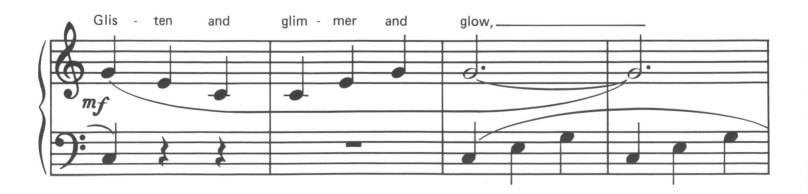

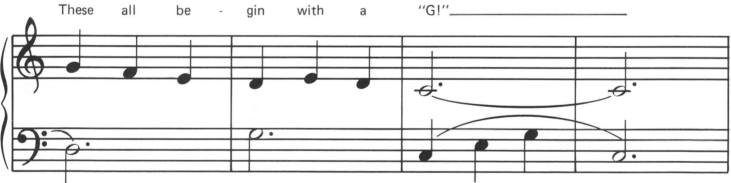

Much slower

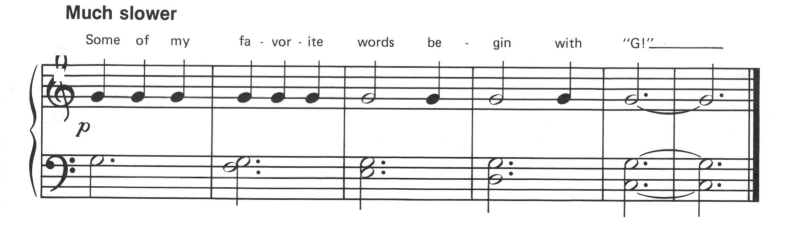

Use after JINGLE BELLS (page 51).

Hymn of Praise

G POSITION

*Based on the chorale
"LASST UNS ERFREUEN," 1623.*

Use after WILLIE & TILLIE (page 53).

Come Buy My Balloons!

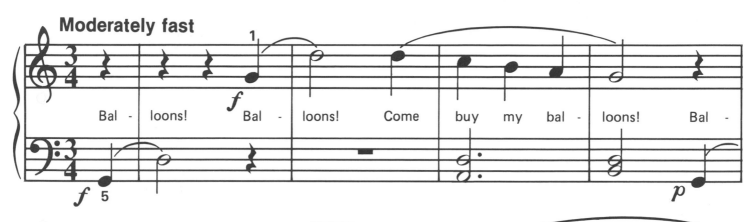

Much slower!

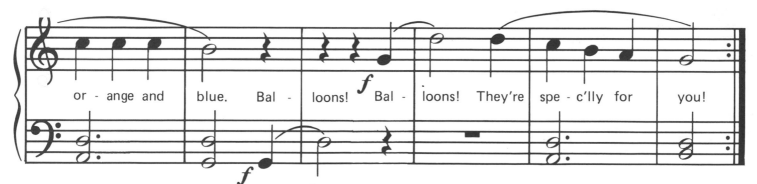

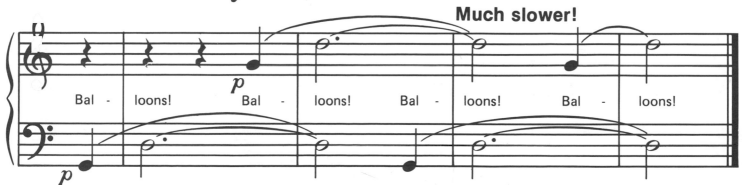

NOTE: The repeat may be taken with the L.H. playing one octave higher, if you wish.

24

Here's a great old folk song that's easy to play, even though the L.H. is in G POSITION and the R.H. is in C POSITION! That just means more fun!

Use after A FRIEND LIKE YOU (page 54).

Who Built the Ark?

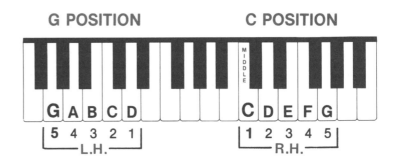

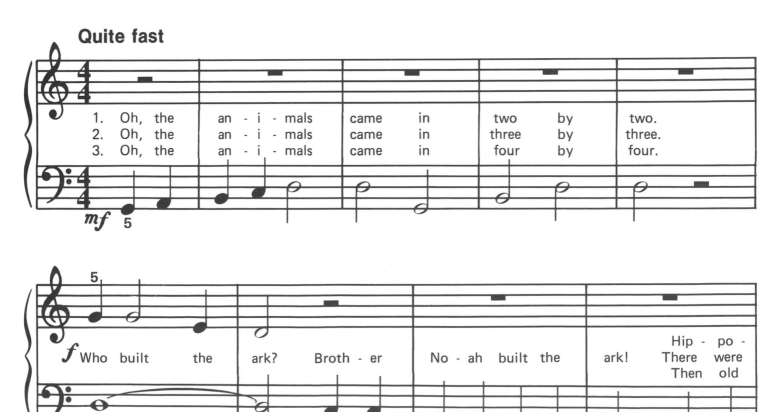

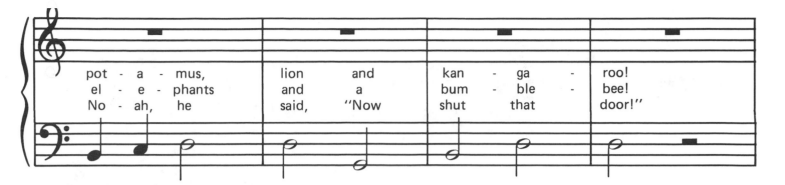

pot - a - mus,   lion   and   kan - ga -   roo!
el - e - phants   and   a   bum - ble -   bee!
No - ah, he   said,   "Now   shut   that   door!"

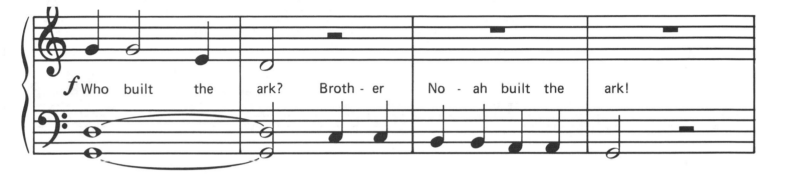

f Who built   the   ark?   Broth - er   No - ah built the   ark!

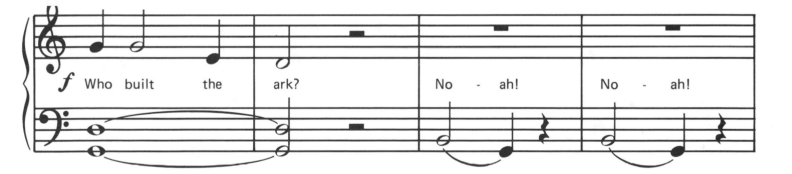

f Who built   the   ark?   No - ah!   No - ah!

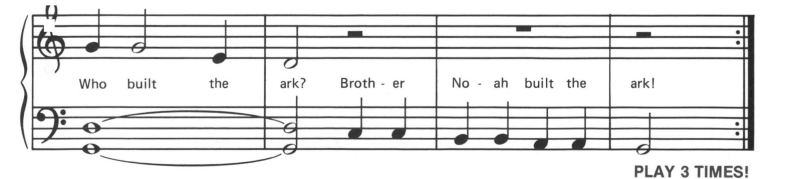

Who built   the   ark?   Broth - er   No - ah built the   ark!

PLAY 3 TIMES!

OPTIONAL: For recital performance, after playing the entire song 3 times,
               play the last 2 lines again, softer, fading away at the end.

A Riddle (Tumbalalaika)

Use after ROCKIN' TUNE (page 56)
or INDIAN SONG (page 57).

C POSITION

Traditional

Moderately fast

f-p

1. Maid — en, — tell me a - gain,
2. Young — man, — why ask a - gain?

What — can — grow with - out rain?
Stones — can — grow with - out rain.

What — can — burn for long years?
Love — can — burn for long long years.

What — can — yearn with - out tears?
Hearts — can — yearn with - out tears.

Use after RAINDROPS (page 58)

The Popcorn Man

Brightly

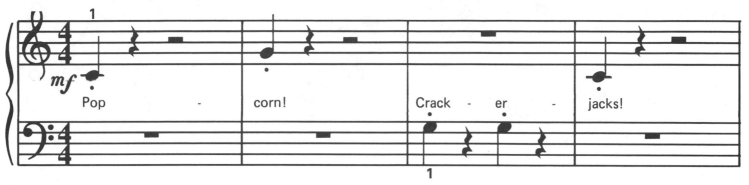

Pop - corn! Crack - er - jacks!

Buy them! Try them! Hot and fresh and good! I'm sell - ing

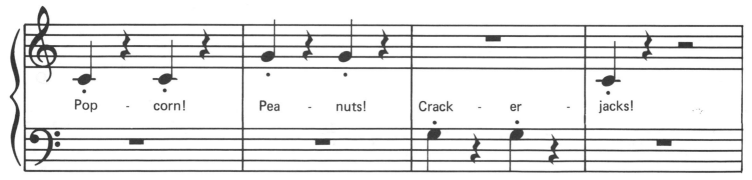

Pop - corn! Pea - nuts! Crack - er - jacks!

Can - dy! Hot - dogs! Ev - 'ry kind of food!

Repeat with both hands 1 octave higher,
if you wish!

Use after IT'S HALLOWEEN (page 59).

Charlie, the Chimp!

C position

Moderately fast

mf 1. Now   I will tell a   tale,   Most pe - cu - liar
2. Now   that you've heard this   tale,   This pe - cu - liar

tale   of a chimp named   Char - lie - Boy,   He could
tale   of the chimp named   Char - lie - Boy,   Go and

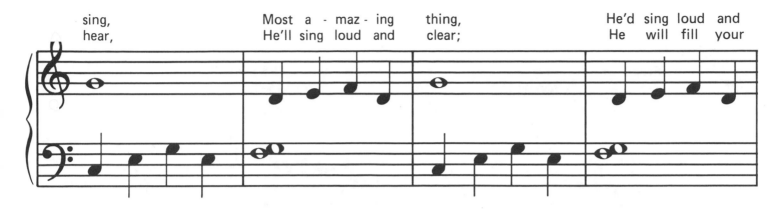

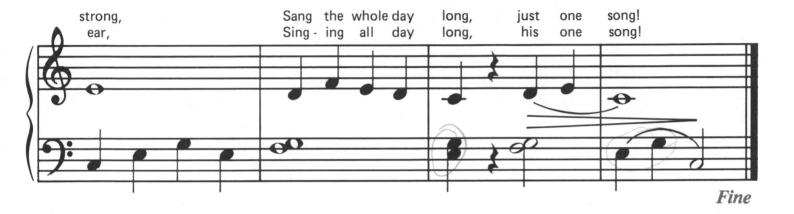

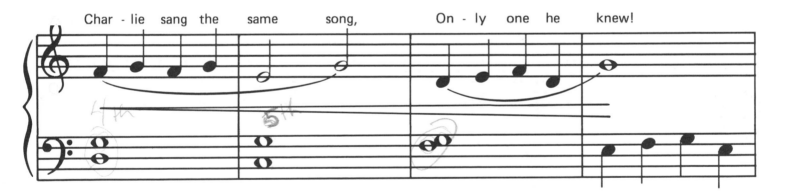

*Use after HORSE SENSE (page 60)
or with the beginning (review section)
of LESSON BOOK 1B.*

This is "MIRROR MUSIC!" The left and right hand move in the same intervals,
but when the right hand goes up, the left hand goes down, and vice versa.
The fingering is the same for both hands, through the entire piece!

My Secret Place

G POSITION

Mysteriously

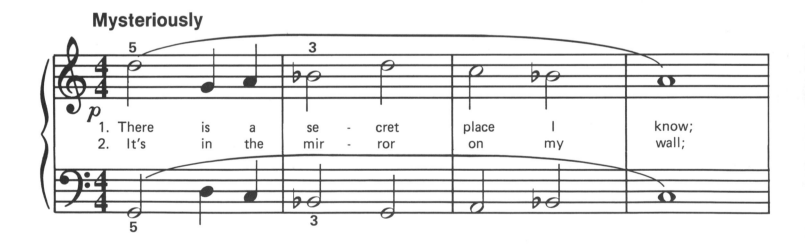

1. There is a se - cret place I know;
2. It's in the mir - ror place on my wall;

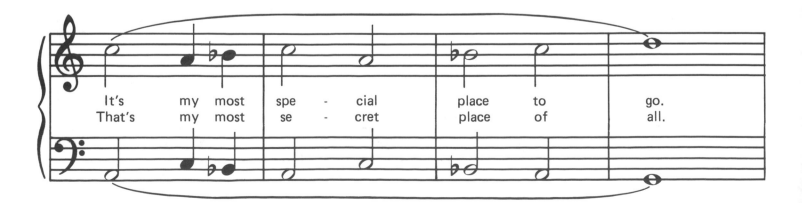

It's my most spe - cial place to go.
That's my most se - cret place of all.

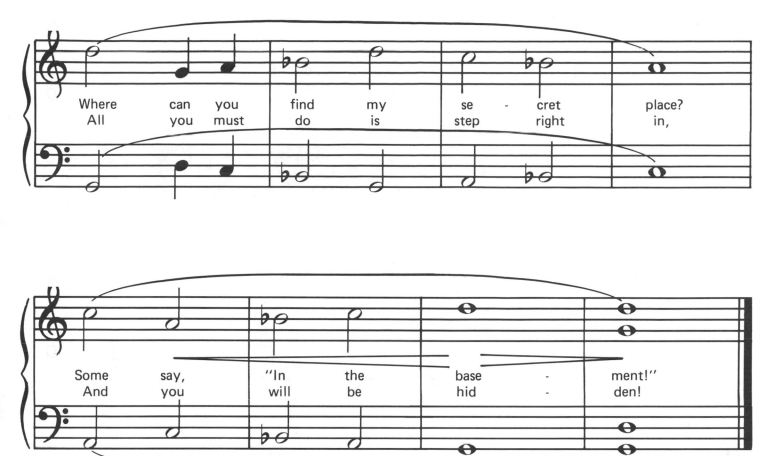

Where can you find my se - cret place?
All you must do is step right in,

Some say, "In the base - ment!"
And you will be hid - den!

Fine

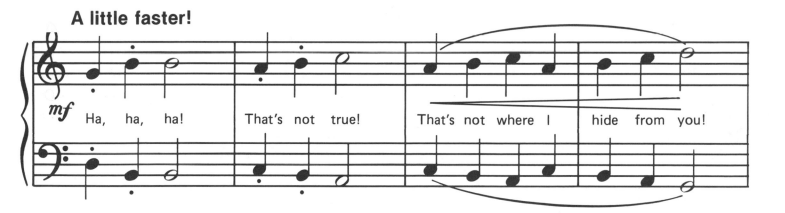

A little faster!

mf Ha, ha, ha! That's not true! That's not where I hide from you!

Slower

f Ha, ha, ha! Now I'll say Where I go to get a - way: *p*

D.C. al Fine

Use after HORSE SENSE (page 60)
or with the beginning of LESSON BOOK 1B.

PASTORALE is a title often given to music that pictures country scenes, particularly *shepherd scenes.* Pastorales are quiet and flowing, and may be played at any season, but are especially appropriate at Christmas time.

Pastorale

C POSITION

Moderately slow

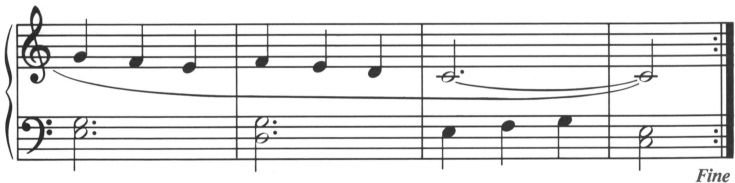

Fine

D.C. al Fine